Journey into the Unknown

The Mystery of the Out of Body Experience

By D.V. Nobles

ISBN: 0-9675704-1-7
ISBN-13: 978-0-9675704-1-9

For my wife, Susan, who listens to all my strange ideas, plans and hopes for the future and still loves me.

Table of Contents

Introduction

One day in November of 2014, something strange and interesting happened. I woke up as normal and went to the room in my home which I normally use as my office. I paused just inside the doorway to turn on the light. I tried flipping the light switch on and then sensing something was wrong, I tried flipping it the other way. I was having some difficulty with the switch and that confused me. I began moving forward into the room towards my desk and chair, but somehow stumbled and fell slowly to the floor.

As I came to rest in an almost weightless sort of way on the floor, I felt like my body was tingling all over. I began to get scared because I did not know what was happening to me. I thought that something was very wrong. As I lay there on the floor, my brain raced with the possibility that something was wrong with me medically. Was I having a stroke? I knew my wife was at work. How could I call her, or anyone for that matter, to get help?

I need to get up, I thought. Almost immediately, I stood back up. It was not like someone would normally get off the floor, pushing with their hands and using their legs. It was simply like I moved from the horizontal to the upright position with no effort. It was then that I started moving back towards my bedroom. This was not my choice. Something seemed to be *pulling* me in the direction I was going.

As I moved across the hall between one doorway and another, I realized that whatever was moving me, my feet were not involved. I had the realization that I could simply jump up a little and I would be floating. So I did. Now as I floated across the floor, a mixture of happiness and fear washed over me. I was overjoyed because I now knew that people could actually float if they wanted to. It was like something I had always known was possible and had not understood how simple it was. However, the fear that was continually growing in me now was the awareness that I was being pulled by *something*. Not only was I being pulled by something or someone, I also knew that I was being brought to meet whoever or whatever that was.

Again, my thoughts raced. Who or what was I going to meet? My fear caused me to conjure up visions of meeting up with some supernatural power or perhaps even an alien. After all, what entity was it that might have the power to pull me weightless to some yet unknown destination? I was now heading back through my bedroom and towards a wall and I instinctively knew that I was also going to pass through that wall. The fear completely enveloped me and I refused to go any further.

My eyes snapped open. I was alone, lying on my bed. One question prevailed among the different emotions I was feeling: *What on Earth had just happened to me?* I lay there for some time trying to make sense of it. This was like nothing else I had ever experienced. In the past, I had strange dreams, lucid dreams and even sleep paralysis. This was something completely different. This was like I consciously got out of bed, experienced these strange things, had cognitive thoughts while experiencing them and was suddenly back in my bed.

After I got up and went into my office room (again), somewhat shaken, but excited, I continued thinking about the experience. The only way that I could describe what happened was by what some call *'Astral Projection'*, or *'Out of Body Experience (OBE)*. My mind flooded with questions. Was this really some sort of out of body experience? Why did it happen to me? How did it happen? Was this experience repeatable and, if so, should I even try to do it again?

I had a lot of questions and I desperately wanted answers. I started researching and combing the Internet for possible clues. The more I searched, however, the angrier I became. As far as I could tell, there were no serious studies on record for this type of experience. Astral Projection was a topic placed into the category of *paranormal science*. This, to me, meant that mainstream scientists shunned the topic completely and I would probably not find any serious information on it. The answers I needed would have to come from elsewhere.

I began looking for others that may have had similar experiences. For the most part, I was not happy with what I found. Although there appeared to be some common threads as to what happens to people during these experiences, there was also a wide range of conjecture and personal beliefs in the mix. I found a collage of fear, unsubstantiated claims, proclamations of enlightenment and harsh warnings from those willing to speak on the subject.

During these weeks of my early research, I had more 'out of body' experiences. I had a deep need to talk to someone about what was happening to me. I thought that there must be someone out there who could relate to what I was going through. Someone must have the answers to my questions. As time went on, however, I realized that no one could provide me with the definitive answers I sought. Other people's experiences, although interesting and, at times, similar to my own, did not explain why this was happening to me. They did not have the answers I so desperately needed. This was a journey that I would have to take on my own.

The reason I decided to write this book is for those who find themselves in a similar situation. I was not a 'new age' person. I was not attempting to reach a higher awareness or enlightened state. I consider myself to have an open mind, but I have an innate need to find logical reasons for extraordinary events. I have a natural curiosity for unexplained phenomena, but I don't blindly accept general consensus as the undeniable truth. I need a measure of proof that will at least satisfy me if no one else. But most of all, I needed information from someone I could relate to. As I said, science was not very forthcoming with answers and those that claimed to be 'enlightened' all had very different views. They definitely appeared to be on a higher level, insofar as they had hundreds of experiences and could not relate to what was happening to me.

It is my hope that if you have recently experienced this, I will provide you with at least some of the answers that you need right now. If you haven't experienced it, are considering it and wondering what it is really all about, I hope that this book will give some insight on what to expect as you move forward in your endeavor into the unknown.

Chapter 1 – Learning to fly

At least circumstantially, it was easy for me to deduce what may have caused my strange experience and how I might duplicate it. A number of things happened that first morning that were outside of my normal routine. These are as follows:

1. When I awoke, I went to my desk as normal and turned on my computer to start my day. After about 15 minutes, I realized I felt sleepy and decided to go back to bed and lay down for a while. This was something I never do.
2. For some reason, when I got back in bed, I laid on my back. This was also something I never do. Earlier in my life, I experienced sleep paralysis, which we will discuss in chapter 2. To avoid these, I was in the habit of not sleeping on my back.
3. Once I was in the bed, I positioned my hands and feet in a very specific way. I pointed my feet inward, one foot overlapping the other and touching. I rested my hands on my chest, palms down and one hand below the other and touching.

I do not have an explanation as to why I positioned myself this way.

Knowing that these were the things I did before the first experience, I reasoned that I might have a chance of it happening again if I duplicated those steps. It did not take long to realize that I was right. As long as I took those exact same steps, I found that I could repeat the process. Furthermore, I discovered that my 'window of opportunity' was between 9am and 10:30am. I could move that time range up a little, perhaps starting an hour later, but generally this seemed to be the optimal time to allow the experience to happen.

Before I go into further detail in my quest to experience and learn more about what exactly was happening, I feel it is necessary to give some background on what I knew of 'astral projection' or 'out of body' experiences prior to having my own.

More than a decade before having my experience, I became interested in astral projection for a very brief period. I probably read something about someone having an experience or perhaps saw it on television. I decided it was worth a try, even though I knew very little about it and was skeptical.

I can remember lying in bed at night, imagining myself lifting from my body. I visualized the image of my physical body still in bed while I floated upwards. Eventually, I saw the top of my house and then the growing landscape beneath me. I believe I did this for a number of nights, but probably not more than a week. I can remember one specific time where I visualized myself rising above my house and moving out towards a nearby lake. I drifted high overhead, along the canal and could see the tops of the trees.

I thought that perhaps this was what people were

experiencing – the visualization of traveling out of their body. However, I knew this was a product of my imagination. I was drawing on my own experiences of what I knew existed on the landscape and what things might look like from above. Even so, I wondered if at least one of those experiences could have been astral projection or some form of it. After that brief experimentation, I lost interest in the possibility. It wouldn't be until years later, after I had first-hand experience, that I would realize my earlier attempts were absolutely nothing like anything I could have imagined.

I already knew this wasn't lucid dreaming or sleep paralysis. As you will see in the next chapter, I was familiar with what those were. At 48 years old, I was encountering something previously unknown to me. Not only was it a new experience, I also found it extremely intriguing. I wanted to understand it and to learn as much about it as possible.

With each new event, it seemed I learned a little more. I tried to understand why I saw the places I did. I took a mental note of the things that happened during these travels. Sometimes I would record my account of an experience on video. Later, I started keeping a diary of the events.

It is important to understand that I was not completely convinced that I was traveling to any actual destination outside my body. As far as I was concerned, this could be something that was being completely manufactured by my mind. After all, we know that the brain is capable of some incredible things and we have no scientific proof that one can leave their physical body. As you will see below, however, there are some equally compelling reasons that they are not a creation of the mind.

I realized very early on, that the one thing that I was seeking above all else was proof. I wanted to know for certain whether this 'astral projection' was something my mind was creating or if it was something that it was *experiencing*. I had heard of other people's accounts of visiting people or places and seeing objects that they would have otherwise not known about. I cannot dispute their personal experiences. However, I can't claim them as the truth, either. I needed to seek proof for myself. I really didn't care if I could prove it to others or even the scientific community. I needed to know for myself.

Proof, as it turned out, was going to be extremely elusive. My early attempts at obtaining it was to try to visit a friend's house and view a never before seen object or to travel back in history to solve a mystery that is yet to be unsolved. Not only were these attempts met with failure, they also appeared to be impossible. For example, each time I tried to travel to my friend's house, I would be diverted to some other place.

Some who are familiar with astral travel claim that you do not actually travel in the physical plane we exist in, therefore obtaining such information is impossible. Still others claim they have visited friends and relatives that currently exist and have accurately identified their surroundings. But, as we will see in chapter 4, most agree there is an infinite storehouse of information available to those who travel. If this is the case, then one would think proof would be easy to obtain.

For the time being, all I could do was try to make some sense of what was happening to me in this new environment. This was of extreme fascination to me as it seemed each new experience brought forth more pieces to the puzzle that I could try to fit together. Below, I have listed a number of events or experiences that became noteworthy during my otherworldly adventures.

- **Perceptual thought and active decision-making:** One of the first and most important things that I noticed which became an endless source of amazement for me was that I could have *cognitive thought* during the experience. For example, if I decided beforehand that I would try to visit a friend's house, then during the experience I would think, *Oh, I need to try to visit my friend's house*. Or I might remember that I need to visit a friend's house and then *decide* to try to do something else first. The fact that I could make active decisions during the experience is quite interesting to me.
- **Difficulty navigating without a physical body:** One would think that if your brain is creating some sort of dream environment, you would be able to move easily around in it. In the beginning, this wasn't the case. Sometimes, I found myself tipping forward as if not sure of how to handle a non-physical body. With subsequent experiences, I learned how to stabilize and move more freely.
- **Learning from one session to the next:** As mentioned above, the process of navigating my environment was a learning process. Each time, I gained more skill and confidence in my abilities. This necessity to learn how to adapt to your environment as well as gaining proficiency over a number of practices does not make much sense if the environment is a product of your own creation.
- **Unknown environments and people:** In normal dreams, your subconscious creates some interesting landscapes. However, quite often these landscapes are constructed with actual people and places from our memory. With the out of body experience, I only encountered unknown people and places, except for seeing my own home

as I traveled away from it. I call this 'new information'. This is information that has to be either entirely created by the brain or experienced by it. To me, it does not make much sense for the brain to create an entirely new environment without using pieces of known environments from memory.

- **See through objects**: To my surprise, as I floated up towards the ceiling of my home and looked at it, I could see a confusing montage of different materials. I could see the material that made up the wood underneath it. Beyond that, I could see the wooden rafters. Other times, I saw through my bedroom into the next room and also to the outside yard. During one experience away from my house, I walked up to a wall and when I reached a certain distance from it, I could look and see what was on the other side.
- **Appearance of the physical body:** It was only my third time out that I became curious and decided to look at my hand. What I saw appeared to be a white outline of my hand, but it was also transparent. Another time, I looked at my legs and noticed they started to dissolve away as I watched.
- **Inherent knowledge (mood or knowing things):** Some places I travelled to would give off a definite 'vibe'. For example, I was filled with a feeling of dread during the visit to one place. In another, there might be a feeling of sadness or elation. There appeared to be no readily apparent reason for this; it was just inherently known. I have also encountered people and would have knowledge of their role. For example, I encountered a man on an island and understood that he was the leader of his people.

- **Window of opportunity:** Probably one of the main reasons I did not have these experiences earlier in life is that I never went through the steps noted at the beginning of the chapter. Most important of these steps, I think, is the specific time in which the experience occurs. This time undoubtedly varies among different people. One thing that seems to be consistent is that your mind must be rested.
- **Lack of sleep inhibits the experience:** I found that I could not invoke an experience before I normally go to sleep at night. I also noticed that if I do not get enough sleep during the night, I will not be able to have an experience. The only thing that happens in this case is that I fall asleep and dream.
- **Increased conscious awareness:** After a number of experiences, I was surprised to find that I felt fully conscious during the exact time when I started 'leaving my body'. This was such that I've often thought, *This can't possibly be happening now, I'm still awake!'*
- **Physical body awareness:** Often during my travels, I am fully aware of my physical body. I can hear my breathing and sometimes, if I'm breathing through my mouth, feel the need to wet my mouth with my tongue. Of particular interest is the fact that I often am aware of a rumbling in my ears during the OBE. I can reproduce this outside of an OBE by concentrating a movement of muscles in my ear regions, although only for a second or less. I suspect that this has some integral meaning having to do with either the cause or the result of having an OBE.

- **Environmental interaction:**
    - **People -** During my very first travels, I did not encounter any people. It was only later, when I made an effort to notice if there were people around that I saw them. I feel that they were always there, if it was an environment that would normally have people in them. I simply didn't notice them because I was so enthralled with this new thing I was experiencing. I could not interact with these people because my role appeared to be that of a visitor to the environment, not part of it. It was only later that I would attempt to seek out an interaction with beings that appeared to be in the same plane of existence that I was currently traveling in.
    - **Places and things –** Very rarely did I interact in any physical way with the environment I was traveling in. The reason I decided to examine my hand was because I was looking at an object (a container) and decided to put my hand on it. Another time, I picked up a butter knife to try to read the inscription on it.
- **Reading:** Many people cannot read in dreams, including me. Whenever I encounter text during my travels, I make a point to see if I can read it. I can read it every single time, although I don't always remember what it said after the experience.

As you can see, I was able to make a number of important personal observations on my own. This gave me some comfort in my attempt to understand the truth behind what I was experiencing. In some ways, I felt like a detective gathering clues in an effort to piece them together. If I could not find the proof I was looking for, then at least I could gather as much evidence as possible. If no suitable proof could be obtained, then I could make a decision based on the nature of the experiences themselves.

My personal observations were important to me because I can trust the information, even if no one else can. As I've mentioned previously, I seek the truth of what the experiences really are for my own benefit. It's also important, however, to consider what might already be known about the phenomenon. In the next chapters, we will take a closer look at what astral projection is and also what it is not.

Chapter 2 – What is Astral Projection?

When we ask the question *what is Astral Projection*, we really have to ask the question, *what is an Out of Body Experience*, or OBE. This is because Astral Projection is just one kind of Out of Body Experience. In this chapter, we will look at the different types of OBE's as well as take the mystery out of some of the surrounding terms associated with travel beyond the physical body.

What is an Out of Body Experience (OBE)?

An Out of Body Experience (OBE) is the act, or perceived act of leaving one's physical body and traveling beyond the physical body's location (bi-location). The description of exactly what part of a person is traveling varies between different cultures and belief systems, but is usually considered to be one's soul. During an OBE, the traveler can perceive many different things. These can include contact with other travelers, visits to yet unknown or unexplored places and travels that transcend the boundaries of both time and space.

An OBE can be invoked in a variety of ways and can be

either self-induced or happen unintentionally, such as a Near Death Experience (NDE). Some other possible ways to have an OBE is through meditation, hypnosis (including self-hypnosis), brain stimulation and hallucinogenic drugs.

A person that has an OBE encounters an alternate perceptive reality other than that normally experienced through the five senses. It is more like an ethereal existence, where the person is not limited to the confines of the physical world. They can observe their own body, pass through walls and other physical objects and travel practically anywhere. The method of travel is usually that of flying, but it can also be instantaneous, traveling from one point to another with no apparent need to traverse the distance in-between. If a person is stationary, they can usually be described as floating, or hovering. There can be a sensation of walking as we do in the physical world, but this is usually during initial OBE's and changes quickly as the person gains more familiarity with the environment.

The out of body non-physical form of the practitioner starts out as something similar to the physical body, with apparent arms and legs and with eyesight similar to that we have in the physical world. During an OBE, if you look at your non-physical body, such as your hand, you may perceive it as being solid, invisible or even a form of energy. After multiple experiences, however, many report that the appearance of the physical body eventually fades away and is replaced by a single point of light or energy. One's visual perception also gradually changes to reach a point where you can see in all directions at the same time. The reasons for these changes are based on the fact that we have lived all of our lives in the physical world. We are quite accustomed to the appearance of physical objects, including our own bodies and we are well aware of the limitation of our peripheral vision. Once placed in an environment where we do not have these limitations, it takes some getting used to.

What is Astral Projection or Astral Travel?

Astral projection, also known as astral travel, is a form of OBE in which a person travels apart from their physical body and usually denotes the separation of the soul from the body. The soul is said to travel through different realms, or different planes of existence. Those who practice astral projection believe that their travel can encompass higher and lower planes of existence. In some cases, this is said to be different levels of heaven and hell or otherwise spiritual places. For others, the travel is multidimensional, having more to do with the construct of the universe, or parallel universes rather than spiritual realms.

What is the Astral Plane or Astral World?

Although the term varies through history and different belief systems, the astral plane is generally thought to be a plane of existence populated by celestial spheres. The term 'astral plane', even though it sounds as if describing a single place, is actually used to describe a number of levels, or planes, of existence. The soul is said to travel through these planes of existence, via the astral body, on its way to being born and also after the death of the physical body.

What are the Akashic Records?

The concept of the Akashic records is that of a vast repository of information that can be accessed on the astral plane. The records are said to contain all history (past, present and future) of events, thoughts and emotions that have existed or ever will exist. Today, the records are believed to available to astral travelers that learn how to access them on the astral plane. It might be argued that since there are many who claim to access these records, some useful or productive information could be retrieved and related to others. The origin of the records stems from the Buddhist belief that a type of permanent record exists in the *Akasha*, a Sanskrit word for 'sky', 'space' or 'luminous' and that of the possibility that the records could be read by man.

What is Etheric Travel?

Etheric travel differs from astral travel in that it can be described as a place more closely related to our physical universe. This can include journeys into our physical world as we know it, visiting actual places and people known to exist on Earth. It can also include travel to unknown places, perhaps even parallel worlds or abstract places, but these places generally conform to what we know of the physical world and adhere to the laws of physics in the known universe. For the most part, this is the type of travel I experience, although it is usually difficult or rare for me to visit known places on Earth. The environments I encounter are mostly Earth-like, presumably existing in another time, planet or parallel world.

What is the Silver Chord?

The silver chord is a tethered connection between the physical body and the soul or 'astral body' while traveling during an OBE. According to most accounts, the silver chord is visible and appears as a thin web-like lattice structure which is connected to your navel region. It is infinitely elastic in that you cannot 'stretch it too far' during your travels. I have looked for this chord while I was traveling and so far have not seen it. However, many people claim they have seen it. It could be that it is associated with the 'astral body' and I have not seen it because I am an etheric traveler. One of the things that is so fascinating about OBE's are the similarities of certain key features reported amongst various travelers. Why do people report being tethered by an ethereal chord? What is the significance of such a thing if it is a dream-like environment created solely by the mind?

What is a Near Death Experience (NDE)?

Many people have probably heard stories where someone has clinically died during an operation and was revived to later tell about a number of things they experienced during their death. Some of the common things reported by people who have had an NDE are:

- A feeling of being at peace
- Moving through a tunnel towards a white light
- Experiencing a review of their life
- Encountering beings of light
- Encountering loved ones
- Floating above their physical body and seeing the operating room personnel

It's interesting to note that an NDE has similarities to normal OBE's such as floating above one's body and being able to see the scene below. However, the Near Death Experience seems to be more specifically related to the final departure of the physical body. Experiencing a review of life, moving through a tunnel towards a white light and the feeling of finally being at peace are not normally found in other types of OBE's.

So now we know a little bit about the terminology and how the different experiences generally relate to having an OBE. But what does it mean exactly to have an out of body experience? And how does this experience differ from other things you might experience like dreaming? In the next chapter, we will take a look at a few of the different states of mind that might be encountered and how they compare to the out of body experience.

Chapter 3 – Maybe it was only a dream?

How does one know if they are having an Out of Body Experience? It may seem like a strange question to ask, but those who have never had an OBE really don't know what to expect. As I mentioned in Chapter 1, when I briefly experimented earlier in life, I was not sure if I had truly experienced an OBE. I found out later that having an OBE is such a profound experience that it will leave little room for doubt. In other words, it is safe to say that you will absolutely know it when it happens. Still, there are a number of interesting phenomena related to sleep that may be confused in some way with an OBE. It is helpful to look at some of the more common ones to understand what an OBE is not.

Dreams

In dreams, we have the possibility to fly and visit some extraordinary places, so why wouldn't this be a form of OBE? Well, dreams are usually the result of our memories – people we know, places we have been and other events – that have happened throughout our life. Dreams also take place during a level of deep sleep where our ability to reason with conscious thought is subdued. We cannot normally make active decisions or observations during our dreams. Dreaming is like being in a movie where the action is being played out. We may be part of the action or watching it, but it continues to play out in ways that doesn't seem predictable.

There are many people who believe that our souls leave our bodies or we astral project while sleeping, but we are unaware of it. I do not believe this is the case at all. Normal sleep and dreams are a way for us to obtain the mental rest we need. It is also a way for us absorb and resolve problems and conflicts that occur during our waking hours. The nature of dreams precludes the possibility of having an OBE during them. However, depending on your sleep state, it is possible to have an OBE after dreaming or transition from a dream to an OBE.

During an OBE, not only is your perception of the environment much like it is when you are awake, you also have a measure of control on where you go, what you see and what happens to you. Instead of seeing these things and only having an emotional reaction as you do in dreams, you are able to consciously consider what is happening. Only after you wake up from a dream, can you ask questions about what you saw or did. During an OBE, you can ask those questions *as it is happening*.

It is possible to start having an OBE while you are dreaming. This depends on the person's sleeping habits and when they might normally have an OBE. It is also possible to *dream* about having an OBE, although it will not be an actual out of body experience. For example, if someone has been trying to learn about OBE's by reading books, watching videos or otherwise immersing themselves in the fascination of the subject, their dreams might be affected by it. One way to tell if the experience is real or a dream is usually the dream will contain imaginary elements only found in dreams. If you are flying around in a forest and you encounter a talking animal, chances are you are only dreaming that you are having an OBE. The experience will also be absent of the 'vibrational' or 'lifting out' stage that is experienced before leaving the physical body.

To further complicate matters, from my experience it is also possible to have an OBE that is *mixed* with dream elements. There are those who believe you have a physical conscious as well as an out of body conscious. Theoretically, your physical brain could be dreaming while the traveling conscious is experiencing other things. I prefer to think, however, that we only have one consciousness and that it is capable of experiencing more than one level of perception. Furthermore, since all of these phenomena occur in various states of sleep, it stands to reason that there can be the possibility of a mixture of them. Ultimately, it is up to the person having the experience to determine what type or category it belongs to.

Lucid Dreams

Lucid dreaming brings us much closer to the OBE, as the person has a level of control within the dream. They are also in a state of consciousness that is closer to the middle ground between being asleep and awake. This is what allows them to have a level of control and to have a measure of conscious thought during the dream. However, like dreams, the environment they experience is composed of people, places and memories accumulated during their life. Also, like normal dreams, lucid dreams have fantastical elements that are a tell-tale sign the person is dreaming.

Similar to the normal dreams above, there is the

possibility to launch into an OBE from a lucid dream state, as well as having a lucid dream about having an OBE. In fact, many claim it is their standard practice to go into a lucid dream as an avenue to start their out of body experience.

Sleep Paralysis

Imagine lying in bed, resting your head on the pillow, but not asleep. As you gaze slowly around the room, you hear a song playing softly on the radio. Suddenly, a nightmarish figure jumps on top of you and with inhuman strength, pushes you down into the bed. You try to struggle, but it only causes the strong arms to force you harder against the bed. You are too terrified to scream and you can't move. In a demon-like voice, the creature demands you either do what it asks or die.

This is what happened to me while in the military. The hours I worked were unusually long and I rarely got enough sleep. When my stress levels were at their highest, I experienced this sleep paralysis episode. This was not my first encounter with sleep paralysis. A few years earlier, while still in high school, I had a number of sleep paralysis episodes.

Those who have experienced sleep paralysis or 'night terrors' will agree: it is one of the most terrifying things that can happen to you. The experience can be almost indistinguishable from reality. You are unable to move due to muscle atonia, a condition normally induced during REM sleep to prevent one from physically acting out their dreams. You may also feel like your heart is beating extremely rapidly. A sense of an 'evil presence' in the room may be felt and you may encounter manifestations of that presence.

In earlier times, sleep paralysis was sometimes called

the 'old hag' syndrome due to the feeling of an evil witch character sitting on one's chest. In more recent times, the evil presence can be a demon, alien or other threatening creature. All of this adds up to an extremely terrifying experience.

Sleep paralysis normally occurs before awakening or soon after going to sleep. It most commonly happens while sleeping in the supine position (lying on one's back). The reason for this may be because the soft palate located in the throat collapses during sleep and obstructs the airway. This causes the lungs to work harder to try to get air, which in turn causes microarousals, or brief awakenings. For those suffering with sleep paralysis, it is also helpful to lessen the stress factors in their life as well as get a healthy amount of sleep.

In the case of my episodes of sleep paralysis, I found that I could move my foot back and forth somewhat. Eventually, this would bring me out of the paralysis. With some trial and error, I realized that if I did not sleep on my back, I would not have an episode. Consequently, I have avoided sleeping on my back for most of my life. The fact that I experience OBE's while lying on my back made me think there is a possible link to the soft palate issue, although I now know I can achieve an OBE while in a reclined position.

Many claim to achieve an OBE by first achieving sleep paralysis. In fact, having an out of body experience is one of the three known types of sleep paralysis. However, it is not necessary to experience sleep paralysis in order to have an OBE. Nor is an episode of sleep paralysis itself an OBE. Like lucid dreaming, it can be used as a vehicle to invoke an OBE.

One of the most common suggestions to have an OBE is that the body should be asleep while the brain remains awake. For this reason, the experience is usually not achieved if you are mentally fatigued, having not had enough sleep. For the body to 'go to sleep', you must remain perfectly still while staying mentally aware. When I come out of an OBE, I notice that my body is in an almost paralyzed state. However, instead of the feeling of helplessness, it feels as if my body is wrapped in a type of protective cocoon. I will usually lay still for a while, letting myself adjust properly to the physical reality. Once I start moving my extremities, they feel very much the way it feels when and arm or leg has 'fallen asleep'.

Experiencing mixed states

During the various sleep states, there is the possibility of moving through them in an almost seamless way. This means that you could be having an out of body experience and then move into a dream state or be experiencing sleep paralysis and move into a lucid dream and so on. So if you can have a dream in the middle of your OBE, how do you know which is which? Well, if you understand the factors that make up the various sleep states as defined above, it will help you in your determination. For example, if you experience an OBE and later find yourself in an environment where you seem to be standing instead of floating and you see someone you know or perhaps something improbable happens, then that is probably a dream.

The different sleep states are usually easy to identify, so there is no need to worry too much about moving between them. Just be aware it is possible for this to happen during an OBE. To avoid this, it helps to practice healthy sleep habits. If you are able to reach an OBE while you are mentally fatigued, for example, it is more likely you will slip into a dream state at some point during the OBE.

The Out of Body Experience

Now that we know a little about some of the sleep states that can be confused with an OBE, let's look at some of the factors that can help us determine whether we are having an actual out of body experience or not. In general, an OBE consists three main phases:

1. **Lifting out** - the sensation that you are lifting (or being lifted) out of your physical body.
2. **Traveling** - Floating or flying to various destinations. Movement during this phase can be stationary, slow, fast or instantaneous.
3. **Returning** - The sensation that you are returning to your physical body, either from being automatically pulled back to it or by your own decision to return to your body.

Before the first phase, there are some signs indicating that an OBE is about to happen. Some of the more common symptoms are listed below. Note that the symptoms are different for everyone. You may experience some or all of these symptoms or, if you are like me, you will not experience any of them.

1. **Vibrations** – Probably the most commonly reported symptom. These can range from slight to intense vibrations. These are not physical vibrations, but are perceived before the start of an OBE.
2. **Buzzing** – Many people also report a buzzing sound, which can become unbearably loud before the OBE.

3. **Various noises** – Different sounds can be heard before or in the initial stages of an OBE. This can be voices, sharp noises such as knocking, a gunshot or other loud sounds. This can be quite disturbing if you are home alone because it seems the sounds are coming from within your home.
4. **Rapid heart rate** – You may feel like your heart is pounding in your chest. This is also a symptom of sleep paralysis. Like the items above, this is a perception and not an actual physical symptom.
5. **Movement sensations** – When you start to separate from your physical body, you might experience a number of different types of movement sensations. Normally, this is a type of 'lifting' sensation or the feeling of being lifted.

If you do experience any of these symptoms, it is also possible that they will change or lessen in intensity as you gain more familiarity with having OBE's. Now let's take a closer look at the three main phases of an OBE:

Phase I – Lifting out: The sensation of lifting out of the physical body is one of the most amazing experiences I have ever had, only rivaled by some of the things I have seen and experienced during my OBE's. Imagine your entire body lifting up, oblivious to the confines of gravity. As you move upward, there are a number of quick 'stop-motions' and an energy-like tingling throughout your body. This all happens in a matter of seconds. You will only experience this during an OBE. The lifting out phase does not happen in dreams, lucid dreaming or sleep paralysis.

Some report difficulty during this phase. It can feel like your body is weighted down and cannot be lifted. You may also have the sensation of lifting out only to fall back down into your physical body. During these difficulties, some have asked for help and feel themselves being lifted up by hands from a person that they may or may not see. Still others have found it helpful to imagine a ladder that they grasp onto and pull themselves up. I had one such incident where I was having difficulty in lifting up and I instinctively imagined a pole from above that I held onto and lifted myself up with. Later, I learned that this technique (using a ladder, rope or other object to pull one's self up) was widely used and suggested.

Phase II – Traveling: Once you have lifted out, it is like all confines have been removed from your body. You can float around your room or you can fly at various speeds to wherever your destination may be. Even though you can fly in dreams, normally it feels like you are walking or moving about as you do in real life. During an OBE, it almost never seems as though you are walking. You are always floating or flying. In fact, it was only in my first few OBE's that I felt like I was standing or walking. The more I became accustomed to being without a physical body, the less I used my non-physical 'legs'.

As I mentioned in chapter 1, the travel phase consists mostly of what I call 'new information'. This is travel to never-before-seen environments and encounters with people never met before. In dreams, lucid dreaming and sometimes in sleep paralysis, you will often be in familiar places and see familiar faces. Also, there is a type of illogic inherent to the various sleep states that you don't find during an OBE. For example, in dreams you might be in a car that suddenly flies into the air and then you park it in your bedroom. Then perhaps the car turns into a motorcycle. This type of abstraction does not occur during an OBE. The OBE appears to follow a set of consistent 'rules' for whatever realm you are in. For example, in my etheric travel, the world I see appears to be constrained to all of the physical laws that govern the universe as we know it. The only exception is me, the traveler. It seems I am confined to a different set of consistent rules. I am not affected by gravity, can move through solid objects and travel at the speed of light. However, it seems also I have a very limited ability to interact with the world I am observing. The fact that the laws of physics, such as they are, are *consistent* within the plane in which a person is traveling is noteworthy. If the travel is happening only in our mind, then not only is our mind creating a completely unique and new environment, we are also creating universal constants for those environments. Where would such a set of guidelines or rules come from? Why would they be followed? As we know from our dreams, we are quite fond of bending or breaking consistent rules.

Phase III – Returning: When a dream ends another one may start or we may simply stop dreaming. If we are having a nightmare, it may become too intense and we awake abruptly. During an OBE, however, we can make the conscious decision to return to our physical body. Many times, we will automatically return as the conscious seems to intuitively know when to return.

When you awake from a dream or other sleep states, you are very much aware of the transition between the sub-conscious and conscious states. While you were asleep, you have the perception that your brain was on auto-pilot and you have very little control of your thought processes. However, when returning from an OBE, you do not feel this type of transition. You feel exactly like you are returning to your physical body. There is a change in the level of consciousness, but it is hard to describe. It is almost like you have two conscious brains.

One is the conscious brain you were traveling with and one is the conscious brain you have in your physical body. They communicate with each other as far as passing their experiences along, but each retains their own clarity. While out of body, the traveling consciousness sees and remembers everything in the same way our waking conscious does. However, as I mentioned previously, I do not believe there are actually two separate conscious brains, but that our brain is capable of the separate perceptions.

Returning is very much like transferring from one active conscious to another. You become more aware of your physical body and your physical surroundings. You do not necessarily feel more rested as you do when waking from sleep. However, you may have more of an emotional feeling such as being enlightened, more open-minded or the feeling of being at peace.

Chapter 4 – Why doesn't science care?

"The mainstream scientific community is pretty well-established that the mind is a manifestation of the brain. There is not mental phenomenon apart from brain function."

-Dr. Steven Novel

At first glance, it appears that the scientific world completely shuns out of body experiences and dismisses them as a product of dreaming, hallucinations or overactive imaginations. However, from time to time, there are serious scientific studies done. One of the big problems that science runs into, though, is that there are no measurements available to determine if one is outside of their physical body. If someone is out of body, then exactly which part of a person has left the body? Is it the soul? Is it part of the conscious mind?

Still, there are some concrete measurements that can be made in order to gather clues to the puzzle. For example, a study was done by Andra M. Smith and Claude Messier at the University of Ottawa School of Psychology in February of 2014. The study involved a student that claimed she could have an out of body experience at will. Since it is quite rare for someone to have an OBE on demand, the researchers took advantage of this and prepared a number of tests, primarily using an MRI to determine brain activity during her experience. The result was what they called an "unusual type of kinesthetic imagery". The student's brain showed similar activity to that of high-level athletes vividly imagining themselves winning a competition. During this, the athlete's brain normally shows activity on both brain hemispheres. However, in the student's case, the brain activity was focused on one side.

Another experiment, perhaps the most popularly known in OBE studies, was done in 1968 by Dr. Charles Tart of the University of California. The experiment is *A psychophysiological study of OBE's in a selected subject* also more casually known as the *Miss Z experiment* because the person tested in this case was referred to in the report as Miss Z.

In the experiment, the subject was fixed with electrodes connected to an electroencephalogram (EEG). While she slept in a closed room, she was observed through a glass window. A shelf was placed high above the bed as well as a clock above the shelf. A paper was placed flatly on the shelf with the number 25132 written on it. She was asked that when she had her OBE, to try to read the number and also look at what time was on the clock. For a few nights, she reported that she could not read the number because she was at different places in the room or even out of the room. On the fourth night, however, she returned from her OBE and reported to Dr. Tart the correct number.

After this event, Dr. Tart and a colleague discussed the experiment and decided that one possible way she could have read the number would be to have a sort of collapsible mirror to extend towards the ceiling. Then, to read the number in the dark, she would also need a flashlight to shine on the mirror. Although not impossible, it seems quite improbable for a test subject to devise such means.

About the same time, Dr. Stanley Krippner was also conducting sleep studies in New York. After reading Dr. Tart's report, he decided to try a similar experiment. Instead of placing a number on the shelf, a picture was slid out of a folder onto the shelf so that no one, not even those conducting the experiment, knew what the picture showed. The test subject in this case correctly identified the picture as a sunset.

The old argument that there has been some success in testing this sort of phenomenon, but it is not *repeatable*, is no longer valid. The science world really doesn't know what to make of results like this. The result is that the study comes under criticism or attack, even though it was done by a scientist using scientific methods. Studies like these are on the very fringe of scientific knowledge and this seems to make some very uncomfortable. If it is possible for someone to exist outside of their physical body, then it opens up a huge opportunity for exploration into the world of the unknown.

If we accept that we are somehow able to perceive beyond the known five physical senses, then we might ask:

What part of us is doing the actual perceiving? (How do we see, touch and smell?)

What is the link between our out of body existence and the physical body?

What supplies information to our brain through this experience?

What boundaries or limitations does our perception have?

What boundaries or limitations in travel do we have?

What type of knowledge can be obtained during this travel?

Is this proof of a soul?

How is this related to human spirituality?

What does this mean for humans as a race?

Can these abilities be used in positive and negative ways?

What effect do these abilities have on the person using them?

These are some very big questions that science is not prepared to address and these are only the beginning. We can easily continue adding to the list and each will spawn many more questions within them.

Because science is unwilling and inadequate to address these difficult questions, progress is slow. The area of study is left to the realm of the unknown. For this reason, those who experience OBE's or those who would like to must turn to other, more non-scientific approaches for answers.

The information then comes from two main sources:

- Those who have had similar experiences and/or,
- Self-proclaimed experts in the field - the so-called "New Age" practitioners and spiritual advisors.

Unfortunately, since the information is based on personal experiences, preferences or beliefs in both cases, there is a definite inconsistency to the available knowledge. For example, while one person might claim there are dangers involved in astral projection, another may say there are no dangers at all. One may say having an OBE is the gateway to your spirituality and higher awareness. Another could say that the experience is simply a mental exercise.

To look at the situation in a more positive light, it could be argued that these people, the ones who have actually had first-hand experience, are really the only ones qualified to have opinions and give advice on the subject. It then becomes something of a personal journey that one has to make, taking advice only when it makes sense to their situation and building upon their own experiences to reach their own conclusions.

So, it is not exactly that science doesn't care. It is that science is not currently equipped to confront and examine the ramifications of what happens when the previously assumed impossible now becomes possible. This is especially true when it comes to the intangible qualities of the human experience.

To those of us who have had experiences in this unknown realm, it is severely frustrating that we must navigate these uncharted territories on our own. However, we cannot wait for science to play 'catch-up'. This is why thousands of people experiment on their own every day. We experience, attempt to explain, interpret and reflect on what the phenomenon ultimately means in our lives. If science ever does arrive at a consensus, it may find that it was one that was already reached long ago by those who have put forth the effort to study it first-hand.

Chapter 5 – Myths, fears and questions

When I had my first few out-of-body experiences, I was filled with questions. The few people close to me that I told had their own questions, although they were a bit different from my own. They were either concerned with my mental health or were fearful of my safety as I journeyed into unknown realms. I have to admit, neither concern was very high on my list. As far as my mental health, I did allow myself some trepidation. I wondered what might have changed in my psychological makeup to allow this to finally happen after 49 years. Could there also be some physiological factor such as a hormonal imbalance or some other chemistry change in my body that was helping to drive this? In the end, however, I decided that it was ultimately by chance that a specific set of circumstances allowed it to happen. It could have happened at any time in my life. The question of fear or safety never entered my mind and I was quite surprised when a friend told me of his concern over the possibility of me 'not able to get back to my physical body'. I instinctively felt there was no possibility of this, but it made me think about it. I decided it was best to learn as much as I could about it to be prepared. After all, this was all new to me. It was like learning to ride a bike for the very first time, but no one was there to help you to keep your balance and explain what perils you might face.

As I mentioned in the introduction, I desperately needed answers to the questions that persisted in my thoughts. Much like one might turn to a doctor for some physical ailment, it seemed to me that there should be someone who was an expert in the subject that could be turned to. There are some people out there who are noted for their expertise in astral projection and other OBE's. Many books have been written about the subject. Since no two 'experts' agree, my advice is to find someone who appears to have some knowledge on the subject and check out a sample of their work. If what they say appears to make sense to you and their advice is relatively sound, you might then look further into their teachings. However, because an OBE is such a personal experience, you must realize that not everything any one person says will necessarily relate to your experiences. This is why I say this is very much a personal journey. You have to learn bits and pieces from others, but rely also on your own intuition and experiences to understand what it means and how it might help you.

With those things in mind, I have put together a collection of questions and answers that might help guide you. Keep in mind these answers are culled from the research I have done not only from my own experiences, but from others as well. These are undoubtedly mixed with my own opinions and interpretations of what I have experienced. Use them as a guide to help you to find the answers that make sense to you.

What if I get lost or can't return to my physical body?

Thousands of people experience OBE's every day. There is absolutely no case that I know of where someone who was known to practice OBE's died during the process. In other words, you have the same chance of dying in your sleep as you do having an OBE.

What if I cut the silver chord?

As you might remember, the silver chord is the infinitely elastic chord that is said to tether your astral body to your physical body. Many report seeing this chord, although I have not as of yet. By all accounts, you can travel anywhere and never worrying about severing this chord. You will always return to your physical body.

Is astral projection or other OBE's evil or sinful?

You might ask the same question about dreaming or other sleep-related activities. There is nothing in the Holy Bible that specifically talks about OBE's. There is a passage that some point to as evidence that an out of body experience was known about and also one that mentions the silver chord. I am not sure that these passages can rightly be interpreted as having anything to do with the subject. However, it is our own conduct that can be evil or sinful, no matter where we travel to. I will talk more about conduct during an OBE in Chapter 8. For me personally, it feels like an amazing opportunity to explore and to take a personal journey. I am grateful for the experiences. If you are unsure of what it means to your faith, ask God for guidance and you will be able to decide if it is something you should pursue. I should also mention that there are those who warn against the spiritual dangers of the experience, but they do so out of fear as they provide absolutely no scripture to back up their claims.

What about the 'shadow people' or other dark entities?

I have not personally experienced this, but I know it is something talked about quite often in the world of astral projection. To me, this type of encounter is something that would happen during sleep paralysis, but many of the accounts seem to occur at various other stages. What I do know is that the majority agree that they cannot hurt you or force you to do something that you don't want to do. It is only your fear that will allow them to cause any negative emotions in you.

Is an OBE dangerous?

The only dangers you face are the same that you would face while asleep or dreaming. Just as in dreaming, if an alarm sounds in the 'real' world, it would cause you to come out of it.

Can you be possessed or bring back a dangerous entity?

I personally do not believe that an OBE opens you up to such possessions. However, because I do not fully understand what happens during the process (no one does), I make sure to protect myself before traveling. To do this, I simply ask God to protect me during my travels – the same way one should ask for protection before going on a long trip, going to bed or during their daily lives. There are many who believe you have nothing to worry about, but there are some who will say there are dangers out there. In my (and many others) experience, it is always best not to carry your fears with you as they can manifest into something negative.

Are OBE's a negative or positive experience? What emotions do you feel?

You should enter the experience with positive emotions and again, do not carry your fear with you. If you are fearful and expect something bad to happen, chances are it will. If you are optimistic and looking forward to the exploration, then you should have a good experience. From my own experiences, what I feel most of the time is a sense of awe at the different landscapes and environments I see. There have been a few cases, however, that I have sensed negative emotions surrounding the place I was visiting. In one particular case, I found myself in a place that was becoming so terrifying that I asked God to lift me out of. I was immediately lifted. Always remember that if you do experience something that is causing you fear or despair, you can always ask God for help.

Will I encounter angels, demons or other spiritual entities?

These types of encounters have been reported during astral travel and near-death experiences. I have not had any of these types of encounters during my etheric travel. If this changes, it would be very humbling for me to encounter an angel. I definitely would not want to encounter a demon, but in any case, if you have these kinds of spiritual encounters, it would be a good idea to seek guidance to try to understand why you are experiencing these things and how you should proceed.

Can I travel through time?

By most accounts, travel to any place and any time is possible.

Can I affect or change something that happened or will happen in another time?

There is no data that supports being able to change the past or future, but there's no reason not to investigate these possibilities for yourself.

Can I manipulate physical objects?

The very definition of an OBE is to perceive or exist in an environment that is not the physical world, so if you are able to manipulate physical objects, it will probably be limited.

Can I visit someone I know?

Many claim to so you can definitely try. According to popular belief, you must be traveling very close to the physical realm for this to happen. The person will not be able to see you or be aware you are there.

Can I visit someone who is also having an OBE?

Some claim they have done this. What would be more fun than to meet up with a friend in another plane? If this is possible, it would require that both people are traveling at the same time, are able to find a mutual location and are vibrating in the same frequency (same relative plane).

Should I tell people about my OBE?

It helps to talk about your experiences with someone you trust and that has an open mind. It is even better if you can talk to someone that has had similar experiences that will better relate to what you are experiencing. Those who have not had an OBE or are able to accept the possibility will look for other explanations for what is happening and may even question your mental health.

Is there something mentally wrong with me?

If there is, there is also something mentally wrong with the millions of others all over the world who have OBE's.

I've never had an OBE. Should I?

If you are curious and prone to enjoying an adventure,

then you might want to. If you are very fearful about what will happen, then you shouldn't. If you are mentally unstable or have trouble distinguishing reality from imagination, then you shouldn't.

I've had one or more OBE's. Should I continue?

It really depends on how you feel about it. If you are enjoying the exploration of it and it's not getting in the way of your normal life pursuits, then you should continue. If you are unsure about the experiences or believe they are negatively affecting you in some way, than it is best not to continue – at least until you determine the cause for the negativity or other barriers that may be stopping you.

What is the purpose of an OBE? Can I do any good with it?

There are claims of using the experience to gain understanding, to heal people (including yourself) and to travel to any place and time in the universe. For me personally, I have felt my mind become more open by the experiences and have a deeper feeling of love for everyone and everything. It is important that you explore for yourself and discover what advantages and understandings can be gained from your journeys.

Can only certain people experience an OBE?

Anyone of any age can experience an OBE. The only things that might stop someone from achieving it are certain mental conditions or sleep related issues.

How long does it take to learn to have an OBE?

It varies from person to person, but it is generally accepted that one month is sufficient for someone to experience at least one OBE if they are trying every day.

Once you have learned the best way to achieve it (see Chapter 7), it will be easier for you to refine and repeat the process. You can then have one every day if you like.

How long does an OBE last?

Again, this varies among different people. Not many people talk about the actual amount of time their experience lasts. For me, it takes approximately 45 to 50 minutes of preparation and the experience itself lasts for 10 or 15 minutes, often broken into a number of separate experiences. The longest time I have been 'out there', I would estimate at less than 20 minutes.

Does time pass differently while having an OBE between the physical world and the non-physical one you are experiencing?

There is some debate about this. Many claim that time passes much more quickly in the non-physical realm and therefore you are able to comprehend more happening in a shorter amount of time, relative to the time in the physical world. This is difficult to determine, however, because the things you are experiencing are not always completely linked together and can be somewhat abstract. The telling factor is when you come back to the physical world, notice the time and are amazed at the time difference. For me, there has been some time dilation like this, but nothing that seemed more than 30 minutes difference.

Do you get the same type of rest during an OBE as you do with sleep?

As far as your physical body is concerned, the answer is yes. As far as mental relaxation, there are some that say yes, but I have to disagree. Since your conscious is active and using the same type of cognitive thought processes you use during normal everyday life, this part of your brain is not getting the rest that it gets during sleep. However, the experience often has a way of making you feel refreshed and/or in a more positive or optimistic mood. This relies, of course, on what kinds of things you experience during the OBE, but generally it can be a positive type of enlightenment.

Once I have an OBE, what realm will I end up in? Will it be in the astral plane or somewhere else?

I think it's safe to say that most beginners travel very close to the physical plane in which we live. You will generally start off in the physical surroundings that your physical body is in, such as your home. From there, you might travel down your street or into a nearby city. In some less frequent cases, you may go straight into the astral plane.

Should my eyes be open or closed while attempting to have an OBE?

Closed. You will see with your mind's eye during the OBE. You can also wear an eye mask if the room is too bright.

Chapter 6 – Seeking proof

Why do our non-materialistic experiences evade confirmation and detection by the guidelines setup in the material world of science? Perhaps the answer lies in the limitations inherent within the models science currently use to perform research and study. If something doesn't fall within the materialistic scientific model, it is rejected by scientists as practically non-existent and labeled as anecdotal.

Most people who have an out of body experience accept it as genuine and look no further for evidence. From the time of my very first OBE, I have been seeking a measure of proof to satisfy my own curiosity. My journey so far has been one of personal exploration mixed with attempts to find some type of validation within my travels to the unknown.

Before we look deeper into how to seek proof, we must have a good understanding of what it is we are trying to prove. Let's look at the out-of-body experience as a whole. Do people actually experience this phenomenon? The answer is yes. Just like dreams or other states of sleep, millions of people experience this every day. The big question, though, is when people experience this feeling of leaving the body, are they actually traveling and perceiving something that is not manufactured by the mind? Are they really seeing something in some other location, whether it be a different plane or dimension? As we've seen, some scientific studies suggest that they are. From my own observations, I find it difficult to believe that the mind is creating all of these elaborate environments.

Audacious as it may sound, the very next OBE I had after my 'accidental' one was a quest for proof. If one could travel to any place and any time, why not go back to see how the pyramids of Egypt were built and put that mystery to rest once and for all? Instead of seeing ancient pyramid construction in process, however, I found myself in the midst of a modern day archeological dig site. Nearby there were large construction equipment such as excavators. These were obviously not what would be used in the meticulous work of excavating the site, but were perhaps used to move the bulk of earth away. As I moved around the site, I was astounded at the clarity and detail of what I was seeing. It was a square type of plaza that receded into the ground. I noticed the stone steps at the site, carts full of various types of tools and trees surrounding the site. Even as I was taking all of this in, I was thinking about finding proof that this was a real place. I thought perhaps I could look at one of the excavators and find a serial number or something on one of the tools that I could identify. While I was thinking this, I saw of all things, a butter knife lying in the sand. I examined it to see if it had writing on it. There were five letters stamped on its surface. Since the letters made no sense to me, I assumed it was a foreign language. At the end of the experience, I felt my breathing had become labored and that I should return. There was a brief period of panic as I suddenly realized I didn't know how to return. I thought repeatedly, *return to my body* and within no time I was back.

In subsequent travels, I started experimenting with different ways to find proof of travel. I decided to try to visit a friend's house and identify an object placed in one of the rooms. He told me what room it was in and where it was, but told me nothing about what the object was. Every attempt to travel to his house, however, either caused me to come back from the experience or end up elsewhere. When I finally did arrive at the area where his house should be, it was a different looking house. Additionally, every time I tried to visit the pyramids, I ended up in a land that might be described as Egypt, but with no pyramids in sight. If these travels were a product of my imagination, why couldn't I see the places I wanted to see? It was as if I was traveling to different places on Earth, but this Earth was not quite the same place as the planet we know. There are some theories that etheric travel, although very close to the physical plane as we know it, actually takes place in a different reality. This could be described as a parallel world or, as some believe, an imaginational physical construct of the plane we are visiting. The idea is that we perceive a type of physical reality because our minds cannot otherwise comprehend or relate to what we are seeing. My current thought is that if it is actual travel, it is travel to a parallel world. If it were a place that evades comprehension where we have to substitute visions of our own creation, I think these visions would be more abstract or rely heavily on things we have seen before. They would not be entirely new structures with notable detail.

My current endeavors to seek proof are inspired by the studies mentioned in chapter 4. If this is actual travel, then perhaps my closest connection with our physical world is at the very point I leave my body - my home. With this in mind, I asked my wife to write a 5-digit number on an envelope and place it on the ceiling fan above our bed where I could not see it. If I am able to travel up to the fan and retrieve the correct number on the other side, then I have my proof of travel.

The concept is simple enough, but the ramifications are enormous. If bi-location is possible and we are able to retrieve information at a distance, then most of what science thinks it knows about the human consciousness is completely wrong. It is at that point that the concept of a soul is no longer a hazy or mystical thing, but possibly quantifiable in its existence. At the very least, it gives credence to claims of the soul and afterlife that have been debated for centuries.

During some OBE's, I noticed that there is no ceiling fan as I've floated around the top of the room. I can see the ceiling and even as I am moving out of my body, I am thinking that I need to check for the number, but there is no fan. This has caused me to consider a number of possibilities:

1. The ceiling fan does not exist in the reality I am in. It doesn't matter that it's right after I leave my body or physically close to my body. Once I leave my body, I am entering a separate reality.
2. The ceiling fan exists, but I am blocking it out for fear of proving the bi-locational travel and would have to personally deal with the ramifications of what that means.
3. My sub-conscious is aware that this is not actual travel and therefore is removing the fan, hence removing the possibility of reading the number as incorrect.

Looking at these possibilities one by one, what about the idea that the fan simply doesn't exist in the reality I travel to? This seems to coincide with everything else I've seen during my OBE's. I am not able to travel to familiar places or see people that I know. It appears to be an entirely different environment. If this is the case, then I would have absolutely no possibility of retrieving any information from the physical world as we know it.

The second option is that I am keeping myself from discovering the proof as it may be too much for me to handle at this point. I have to consider this, but I feel it is a somewhat weak possibility. I have no objections of receiving quantifiable proof of the fantastic. Others have already proclaimed they have such proof. Scientific studies have been done offering proof of bi-locational travel. If I do indeed have some fear of proving this for myself, then I must look deeper and resolve that fear before I will be successful.

The last possibility is that I am stopping myself from receiving proof because I know deep down that it is a creation of my mind and I must not want to admit that to myself. When I wondered about this possibility, I had to contemplate in this case why the fan would be missing. If it is my mind stopping me from discovering the truth, why not leave the fan there and just not be able to reach it? Or perhaps it could be reached, but no envelope could be found. Also, why would the fan be absent in previous OBE's, before I even considered this type of test?

The last possibility would mean that I want to accept the OBE as a valid bi-locational experience and wish to continue to delude my mind into thinking so. In my search for the truth, I have to keep this as a possibility. No matter how amazing and detailed the OBE appears to be, I have to consider that it is somehow a product of my mind.

The first and last possibilities are the strongest in my opinion. I am either traveling to environments that are not in our current physical realm or I am not. This creates quite a catch 22 situation as far as obtaining proof. If I am indeed traveling to some parallel existence, it is impossible to find any verifiable proof that coincides with our physical world. Similarly, if I am *not* traveling at all and it is a creation of the mind, I will not find proof.

As an aside, this is the entire problem with proving astral travel. There is nothing located in the astral or spiritual plane that can be verified between the physical and non-physical plane. The only possibility is the Akashic records. If this is truly accessible information that is all encompassing of the sum of human knowledge, then information can be retrieved and brought forward as proof. However, even though many profess to tap into this knowledge bank, absolutely no one has returned with verifiable information. Think of all the mysteries that could be solved with such information.

In subsequent attempts, there were times that the ceiling fan existed. During one attempt, I saw numbers and they were flashing in and out in a very erratic fashion. I was able to get the numbers '5512' or '55', '1' and '2'. When I checked the actual envelope, the number on it was '72951'. I was disappointed, but then I realized that all of my numbers actually existed in the real set of numbers. This encouraged me to keep trying.

A couple of weeks later, I was able to see and reach the fan again, although with a frustrating and erratic side to side motion. Later, I reflected that this might not be motion at all, but rather the problem of trying to perceive in this 'out of the body' realm. I could not read the entire number, but was able to see the number '26'. I was not sure if this was at the beginning of the number or the end, but once I came out of it I decided to check the envelope. The number on the envelope was '87462'. Again, I felt a pang of disappointment. I was holding the envelope by the corner and it suddenly pivoted in my hand, showing the numbers upside down. Reading it that way, I saw the number '26' and raised my eyebrows. Was it possible I was reading it backwards during the OBE? This was not proof by any means to me, but again it encouraged me to keep trying.

The only proof I will accept in this type of experiment is the exact numbers, whether they be forward or backward. I realize, of course, that this would not be scientific evidence. Nor would it be evidence for anyone else, except perhaps to those who know me and trust me as a person of my word. As I mentioned in an earlier chapter, it is something that I need to prove for myself.

Later attempts yielded more difficulty in seeing the numbers or seeing the fan at all. I soon realized that concentrating so much on trying to get the numbers seemed to be forcing me into more of a lucid dreaming state than OBE. I decided to take a break from proof-seeking for a while and go back to enjoying the adventure of the experiences. Allowing myself to have the experiences in a more carefree manner was like a breath of fresh air. The travel and visions came more natural and easier.

If I do find proof of actual travel, I have to consider the amazing consequences of this. What does it mean that we can leave our bodies and go to other places? What is the purpose of this possibility of exploration and what can I learn from it?

If I determine that it is a product of the mind only, then I have other questions. Why does my mind need to create imaginary places to travel to? Why would it create such elaborate new environments when it has a lifetime of memories to build them from? What do these experiences tell me about my own psyche and what should I do about it?

I will continue my search as long as I am driven by the need to understand more about this phenomenon. If I find that my current method doesn't work, I will look for others. For example, I might look around my home while out of body and determine if there is anything similar that exists in both planes. Even if there is, it doesn't guarantee that information placed there (i.e. a paper with numbers written on it) will be able to simultaneously exist in both realms.

Many claim to visit people and places they are familiar with in the physical world. In this case, they are said to have a 'low vibrational frequency'. A higher vibrational frequency, according to many, is needed to move into different planes of existence. The higher the vibrational frequency, the further away a person moves from the physical plane.

In a way, I feel as if I was at this lower frequency with my very first experience. I was moving around in my home, unaware that I was even having an OBE. In my next experience, it seemed as though I already moved up into a different type of etheric plane. Most of my experiences have occurred so far in this 'parallel world' type of plane. Now, I am starting to see indications that it is changing again. Perhaps the next stop is the astral plane of which so many speak about. As far as seeking proof goes, this is unfortunate. I would have liked to stay closer to the physical plane longer so that I could try these experiments. On the other hand, supposedly one can move between the different types of planes at will. So perhaps I will be able to find proof after all.

If you've never had an OBE, you may be reading this with your own thoughts on how to obtain proof. If you are ready for this type of adventure, then leave your fears at the door and prepare for one of the most amazing experiences you will ever have. In the next chapter, we will cover some methods you can try so you can have your own out of body experience and see what this is really all about.

Chapter 7 – How to leave your body

I have purposely put this chapter towards the end of the book. I know that many people are fascinated by the prospect of astral projection or having an out-of-body experience and are eager to learn how. However, like many things in life, it's a good idea to learn more about it before attempting it yourself.

Common sense tells me that I should caution you before attempting this. By most accounts and in my own opinion, trying to have an out of body experience is perfectly safe. However, since no one seems to be completely knowledgeable on the subject, it is a learning experience. Also, everyone's personal health, situation and circumstances are different. If you follow these or other instructions, it is by your own choice and you must use your own judgement if you decide to try this experience.

There is no single method that works for everyone. With that in mind, I am going to provide you with a few different methods you can try. If one doesn't seem to be working, you can try another. It may take some time, but you should be able to find the one that gives you the best results and you will no doubt customize it to work best for you. You can also mix the different methods as you see fit to achieve the best results.

There are a few considerations to keep in mind no matter what method you attempt:

1. **Safety first.** If you are watching children that cannot be left unattended or have other responsibilities that require you to be aware, *do not attempt* to have an OBE. Use your best judgement. Generally, if it is ok for you to be asleep at the time you attempt an OBE, it is safe to proceed.
2. **Make travel preparations.** Have clear intentions in mind on where you want to go and what you want to do during your travel, just as you would travel to any destination. More about this is covered in the next chapter.
3. **Protect yourself.** Although there is nothing known that could cause you real harm, it is possible your own fears will cause your experience to have some bad elements. Since we do not have a full understanding of what is really happening during an OBE, it is always a good idea to keep your fears at bay. I say a little prayer each time before I start my travel. It can be something as simple as "God, please protect me in my travels". Remember that you can always ask for help or return to your body if you run into a bad situation.
4. **Avoid trying to have an OBE when you are tired or sleepy.** If you try, you will most likely fall asleep and dream. This was probably my biggest mistake when I first made my half-hearted attempts years ago. The result was that I concluded it wasn't a possibility and quickly dismissed the idea, missing out on years of possible exploration. Even now, after having many experiences, I still try from time to time when I lay down to go to sleep. The result

is that I prolong the time it takes for me to fall asleep and often drift into an unpleasant area between being awake and asleep. This only causes you to get less sleep which can adversely affect your OBE attempts as well as create many other problems in your life.

5. **Practice healthy sleep habits.** As stated above, lack of sleep is not good. It's ok if you are a little lacking in the amount of sleep you should get, but when you go beyond that it can prevent you from having an OBE.
6. **Eat healthy foods and keep yourself in good physical shape.** Like good sleep habits, the better your eating and exercising habits, the better mental shape you will be in. This can affect the clarity and strength of your OBE's and allows you to make better decisions while having them.
7. **Avoid having an OBE when in a bad mood or depressed.** Like fear, any negative feelings or emotions you bring in will undoubtedly manifest themselves in some way during your experience. This can only add to the stress you were feeling before the experience. Do not attempt to have an OBE if you are mentally unstable or otherwise have issues differentiating between dreams and reality.
8. **You must remain completely still.** I have never practiced meditation, but I'm sure it would be helpful in this case. Your body must reach a certain point of muscle atonia. It does *not* need to be full sleep paralysis. When trying to remain still, you might run into a couple of problems. You may notice some minor itching or other body interruptions like aches or twitching. Becoming aware of little itches is normal because your mind is not distracted with other things. If the itch is

minor, you can completely ignore it. If more bothersome, simply scratch it to make it go away. When you are more experienced, you will find that this only happens in the first couple minutes and sometimes not at all. Once you learn that most of these things can be ignored, they will simply go away. If you have more intense conditions, such as chronic pain or uncontrollable body movement, you will most likely be unable to achieve an OBE unless you are able to mentally ignore the condition.

9. **Relax your muscles.** Often when we lie down and try to be still, we are not aware that we are still tense in some areas. Take a mental inventory of yourself starting from your feet and moving upward. You will usually find that you are using certain muscles to maintain a position. Allow yourself to relax.
10. **Breathe normally.** When you first start, your breathing may be a little erratic. Allow your breathing to be steady. There is no need to try to mimic the deep breathing that happens during sleep. You may also find that you have saliva building up. Just swallow as normal, just as you would if you were awake. This is another thing such as itching that manifests itself simply due to trying to achieve a calm state. These problems will lessen with more experience.

11. **You must clear your mind.** The idea is to not think about anything. However, those who know a bit about how the mind works also know that this is impossible. Thoughts will always prevail. There are a few methods I use and, in fact, these same methods can be used to help you sleep if you have trouble sleeping.
    a. **Put your attention on the darkness you 'see'.** Even with your eyes closed, there is a kind of 'movement' or different shades of black that can be seen as you look at your closed eyelids. You can watch this and allow yourself to become interested in the changing shapes or shades.
    b. **Listen to the ringing in your ears.** For me, this is fairly loud, but it is a constant sound that you can focus on.
    c. **Do not allow your thoughts to fully form.** What I mean by this is that when you think of something, it will cause you to think of something else and so on, causing a full thought pattern. Try to get into the habit of cutting off a thought and letting a separate one appear in its place. If you form complete thought patterns, it will stimulate you to stay in your fully conscious state. What you are going for is a state just between awake and asleep. You will usually have some thought patterns that fully form. This is unavoidable and you will find your mind wandering off thinking about something other than what you are trying to achieve. This is not a problem. You will notice that this happens less as you become more experienced. When you cut

off your thought patterns, your thoughts will seem disjointed. Since this may be a slightly difficult concept to grasp, I will further illustrate below by listing what normal and disjointed thought patterns might look like.

i. **Normal thought pattern:** *Oh, the car is low on gas. I need to stop by the gas station next time I go out. Gas is getting so expensive now. I have to check my bank account to see if I have enough money for the light bill. I wonder if I should change my lights to those new eco-friendly bulbs that...*

ii. **Disjointed thought patterns:**

1. *Oh, the car is low on...*
2. *I really like my new job, but...*
3. *I wonder if the cat...*
4. *I'm going to focus on the darkness and...*
5. *It was so funny yesterday when...*

d. **Alternate your attentions.** As you think disjointed thoughts, you might have the feeling that you are rambling in a non-sensible manner. You may also notice images start to appear and fade. To avoid falling completely asleep, try to alternate between looking at the darkness, listening to your ears ringing or some other constant sound as you are avoiding thoughts to fully form.

12. **Make sure there are no distractions.** If there are people around or loud noises, you won't be able to achieve an OBE. One thing that I usually do is turn off the air conditioner because it is fairly loud when it kicks on. Sometimes I think that I should disconnect the phone, but you never know when there may be an emergency, so I leave it as is. Luckily, I have rarely been interrupted.
13. **Do not duplicate your sleep environment.** I usually sleep with an air filter running as well as a fan during the warmer months. When I prepare to have an OBE, I turn both of these off. If possible, do not lie down, but sit in a reclined position of about 45 degrees (example: the angle of a beach chair).
14. **Stay calm.** When you reach what many call the 'vibrational stage' - the point where you are about to leave your body - it is common for fear or excitement to overcome you. If it does, you will not be able to achieve an OBE. This is not a problem because if you were able to reach that stage, then the hardest part is over. It means you have already determined your method and have the means to achieve an OBE. It is quite exciting when you experience that feeling of leaving your physical body for the first time. In fact, practically every stage of the OBE is new and exciting and may overwhelm you the first few times. During my first experiences, I maintained a sort of tentative excitement because I knew if I let my emotions get out of hand, I would only come back. Once you are 'out there', however, feel free to be awed and freely enjoy whatever visions you have. You will find after the first few endeavors, you will become accustomed to the 'lifting out' stage.

Now we will take a look at the different methods you can try in order to achieve and OBE:

Method 1: The window of opportunity

The idea behind this method is to find the optimal time for you to have an OBE. I was lucky enough to stumble upon my window of opportunity by accident, which is a couple of hours around the early morning. The common denominator with this method is to go to sleep, wake up at a specific time and then stay up for a short time before attempting an OBE. You may have to experiment with different times to find the time that is best for you. Although I don't recommend the time you normally go to bed as a window, some do claim that time is successful for them.

The 'window of opportunity' method focuses on an optimal time in your sleep cycle to assist in reaching the state of mind needed for an OBE. Other methods focus more closely on achieving the specific state of mind needed with less regard to your sleep cycle.

After covering considerations 1 through 14 above, you basically wait until you reach the 'lifting out' phase. There is a common phrase that many use when describing the state you need to be in. That is to have your body fall asleep while your mind stays awake. It only means that your body enters into a state of slight muscle atonia. While you wait, you may feel a tingling in your arms, legs or other parts of your body. Accept this and let it spread throughout your body. Your mind doesn't exactly stay awake, but enters what is called the hypnogogic state. This is the state your mind is in between being awake and asleep. You pass through this state every night while going to sleep. By attempting to keep your mind awake, you are prolonging this state.

Method 2: Waking the non-physical body

With this method, as you enter the hypnogogic state described above, you think about moving a part of your body such as your hand or foot. For example, think about your hand and visualize it with your mind. Imagine moving your fingers, but don't physically move them. Continue doing this until it actually feels as if they are moving. Move to other parts of the body and repeat the same process, each time visualizing each aspect of that part of the body as well as the movements. Depending on how well things go, this could take one session or a number of sessions. Once you feel comfortable in moving various parts of your body, start concentrating on moving a section of your body such as lifting your legs or sitting up. To assist in this, you may also use the 'rope method'. This involves an imaginary rope hanging from the ceiling. With your new found energy limbs, grasp the rope and use it to pull you upwards. All of this is meant to start the 'lifting out' stage.

Method 3: Mental projection and visualization

If you have a good imagination or can easily visualize things, you may want to try this method. It involves visualizing an object with as much detail as possible. Before attempting your OBE, locate an object in another room. It should be something that you have a fairly strong connection to, such as a favorite pen or a gift from someone special. Examine the object from all angles. Think about all aspects of the object, such as the color, weight, shape and even smell. Put some real thought into this, don't just consider the properties in a passing way. You want to become intimately familiar with the object so that it will be easier to recall later.

Walk from the place where you are going to have the OBE to the object. Think about everything you are experiencing as you move towards the object, such as the number of steps, the sounds, the things you are passing by and what you are seeing with your eyes. Pick up the object again and examine it. Do this as many times as you can.

After going through considerations 1 through 14 above, visualize yourself walking to the object and picking it up. Visualize, with as much clarity as possible, all the steps taken to reach the object. Imagine yourself picking up the object and examining it as you did in reality. Consider all the different properties of the object. Feel the weight of the object and look at its size and color. Continue doing this as you move into the hypnagogic state.

Repeat these steps of visualization as much as possible until you reach the vibrational and 'lifting out' stage. If this type of visualization doesn't work for you, you may want to try other visualization or meditative techniques.

You should set aside a couple of hours to attempt any of the methods above. Although it varies, it may take you more than an hour to get to the 'lifting out' stage and the actual OBE may last up to several minutes. Those attempting to have their first OBE may experience it within the first few tries or it may take up to a month. The good news, however, is once the genie is out of the bottle and you have learned what technique works for you, you can easily repeat it. After that, it is possible to experience it every day if your situation allows it.

To get a more intimate view of what happens during the steps of an OBE, see chapter 9, *Anatomy of an OBE*. In the next chapter, we will look at the 'lifting out' stage and what to expect once you break free from the confines of your physical body.

Chapter 8 – Tripping the realm unknown

Once you have determined the best method to use, you will reach the moment of truth – the point where your energy body separates from your physical body. Before this happens, many report experiencing things like strong vibrations, loud noises, hearing their name called or loud buzzing sounds. You may also hear loud pops, banging noises or other strange sounds. This can be quite scary when it first happens. These sounds are so real, you can easily think they are happening in the physical world. If you experience vibrations, they can be so strong you may think something is wrong with you physically. However, none of these things are happening in the physical world and none of them can harm you. You should try to remain calm and allow yourself to separate from the physical body.

For some, this is easier said than done. For others, it is no problem at all. If you feel you are having trouble with the separation, there are some things you can do to assist the process:

- Repeat to yourself, *I am now lifting out of my body or I am now leaving my body*

- Imagine a rope or ladder that your non-physical hands reach up to in order to pull yourself upwards. This is also helpful if you feel your body is 'weighted down'.
- Ask for help! Believe it or not, no matter where you find yourself during your travels, you can always ask for help or ask questions and will always receive some type of response. Many have reported feeling hands lift them upwards.
- If you still can't rise out of your body, you can try to sit up or roll out as if rolling off the bed.

Some report getting 'stuck' at the lifting out stage and give up. The above suggestions should help you get past this. If you still have problems, it may be some measure of fear that is preventing you from lifting out. Remember to keep an open, optimistic mind and look forward to the adventure.

Once you are free from your physical body, you will be in an entirely new environment. You will need to learn how to move around and what to do. Luckily, this is usually quite easy and you will find much of it automatic. Trust your instincts as they will guide you best when you are not sure about something.

As mentioned earlier, you should have a travel plan. All you need to do is think about where you want to go and you will start moving towards your destination. During early OBE's, when I wanted to go somewhere, I would quickly fly over the distance in between. After a time, you will learn that you only need to think of where you want to be and you can appear there instantly.

In the beginning, you will also find that your non-physical body is much like your physical one with arms and legs. You may also have some trouble moving around. This is because you have years of experience in moving around in your physical body. You may try to mimic those movements or even try to walk, but it doesn't work like that in the non-physical world. As you gain more experience in this new environment, you will find that your non-physical duplicate body will fade away. You become more like a point in space with no hint of a physical body. The more you learn about moving, you will find that there really are no limitations. The only limitations you will have are usually created by your own hesitations or fears.

As you travel to your destination or move around in this new environment, you will now be able to truly relate to what others have experienced. Words are really not sufficient to describe it and you will easily understand why. It is almost like being at the brink of the amount of sensation or perception that the mind can comprehend. For me personally, many times I am simply filled with awe at what I am seeing. Once back to the physical world, trying to explain it or writing it down is almost pointless because there is no way to capture the essence of what was experienced.

During your journey, remember that there is nothing that can cause you harm. If you feel threatened or scared, you can always go to a different place, ask for help or decide to return to your body. You might even ask "Why am I experiencing this?" You may find that it represents a fear or problem in your life that you must overcome.

At some point during your exploration, you will most likely return to your body automatically. If, however, you are in the midst of your travels and you feel the need to return sooner, you can will yourself to return. To do this, simply say to yourself, "I am now returning to my body". If you don't immediately return, repeat the affirmation and you will soon return.

Returning to your physical body is very much like waking up from sleep in that you can sense a definite change in the type of cognitive awareness you have. You may want to remain in the same position for a minute and think about the experience as you let yourself adjust to the physical surroundings. When you feel like you want to get up, first move your hands or arms slowly. Your body will most likely still be in a state of sleep, so you might feel some tingling as you move. This very quickly goes away once you move any part of your body.

Depending on what type of experience you had, you may feel like your mind has been opened and you may even have a greater love for those around you and, in fact, for people as a whole. You may also feel like anything is possible and have a more optimistic outlook on life and the things you want to accomplish. It's definitely a form of enlightenment which can help you see things more clearly.

You may want to start a journal to document your experiences. You will find that each session is a learning process. Also, by documenting, you can look for patterns in your experiences or try to determine the meaning behind them. If you find yourself discussing your adventures with others, you will want to be able to refer back to certain experiences to remember details or know exactly when they happened.

Now that you have experienced an OBE for yourself, you will begin to realize that no one person has the answers to the questions you may have. They cannot answer why this phenomenon happens or what it means in our daily lives. Even though we can try to relate our experiences to one another, in the end it is journey that one must ultimately take alone to find the answers we seek.

Chapter 9 – Anatomy of an OBE

When researching how others achieve OBE's, I was amazed at how many list only a few simple steps without really going into detail on what needs to be done or what is happening during those steps. I understand how important these details can be for someone who has little or no experience with the process. In order to further clarify this, it is necessary to look more deeply into the experience. In this way, we might get more insight into the idiosyncrasies that are evident during each phase, which can be difficult to put into words. With that in mind, I offer the following actual experience of my third OBE with as much useful details as possible:

December, 2014 – approximately 2 hours total time, of which approximately 15-20 minutes included the actual OBE.

08:25 am – I wake up from previous night's sleep.
08:45 am – I prepare for OBE by turning off the air filter, heater and anything else that might interrupt the session.
08:46 am – I lay on my back, point feet inward and rest hands on my chest. I decide that the purpose of this OBE is to attempt travel to a friend's house to seek proof of

possible travel. I ask God to protect me in my travels. I close my eyes and start relaxing all muscles.
08:48 am – As I look at the darkness under my eyelids, I try to keep my thoughts from fully forming while I remain fully aware.
09:00 am – I notice a tingling sensation in my right arm. Later I sense the same thing in my lower left back. I allow these sensations to continue through my body. These are indications that my body is 'falling asleep'.
09:30 am – My fully conscious state is transitioning into the hypnogogic state. Thoughts are replaced by brief hallucinations that I am only mildly conscious of.
09:45 am – For the next 40 minutes, I am constantly prevented from full sleep by air being blocked in my throat. As soon as I drift off to sleep, certain muscles in the mouth and throat area relaxes. The soft palate partially blocks my airway and causes a snoring sound which partially awakens me. This turns out to be advantageous because it keeps me in the hypnogogic state. I try to breathe through my nostrils, but always end up breathing through my mouth. After some time, I am able to successfully breathe through my mouth without causing the blockage. I continue in an uninterrupted semi-conscious hypnogogic state. During this time, there is only a vague feeling of being aware of my state of consciousness.
10:25 am – The 'vibrational' or 'lifting out' phase begins. I feel like I am being propelled upwards, leaving my physical body behind. As this happens, it is like I am in a heightened state of awareness compared to my previous hypnogogic state. I immediately remind myself to remain calm as I transfer into the non-physical realm. As this is only the third time I've had an OBE, the 'lifting out' sensation is still quite new to me and very exciting. It is easy to feel overwhelmed by that as well as the

anticipation of what may lie ahead.

10:26 am - I found myself in a dark place. There appeared to be walls or corridors, but they were black and instead of being closed in, it was either a very large structure or out in the open. At one point, I noticed stars in the distance. When I looked at them, I was awestruck. It seemed that I was seeing stars at every conceivable point. There were millions of them. Soon after that, I found myself in an open area that might be described as outer space, although that was not my impression. I let myself relax and float in this area. An inner peace filled me and an indescribable feeling of content washed over me. I wanted to stay there longer, but soon I returned to my physical body. As I did not feel the familiar cognitive awareness of being awake, I waited for the next OBE to start. I estimate the next one started in about a minute.

10:30 am - Although it is difficult to discern how many short OBE's I had or what sequence they were in, I do remember having a conversation with someone. I got the distinct impression the person was a female. After she spoke to me, there was some kind of vocal reply that I needed to convey. For some reason, perhaps out of inexperience, I felt that I needed to reply by speaking with my physical body. This caused me some concern about talking too loudly as it might bring me out of the experience, so I spoke very softly. I was perhaps not aware that I did not need to physically speak at all, but could have responded with my thoughts. I have no recollection of what was said in the conversation. Not only was I unaware of what was said after I returned, I also felt that I was not aware of what was said while the conversation was happening. It was as if someone had a private conversation with a part of my soul that my conscious was not allowed to be aware of. Also, I have no particular emotional memory of the conversation except that it was a necessary interchange and what was said had some importance tied to it. At some point after this, I came back and again waited for the next OBE to start. As before, I did not have to wait long before the next one started.

10:35 am - In my final and longest OBE, I moved within my house. I went out of the bedroom and into a spare bedroom. I perceived opening the spare bedroom door, even though in reality this door was already open. I floated upwards and as I looked at the ceiling, I started to see the different materials it was made of. I then saw the rafters beyond that as well as the wood and material that made up the attic. I was trying to process this information and trying not to get overwhelmed. I then reminded myself that I wanted to try to travel to a friend's house to seek proof of actual travel.

I immediately started flying, but did not notice any points along my route of travel. I was suddenly in an outdoor park and I noticed some music playing. I thought of this as a type of circus music, but cannot be sure. I was confused as to why I was at this place instead of my friend's house and decided to leave.

I moved away from the area. At this point, I also noted that I was having trouble with my orientation. I seemed to be tilting down often and seeing the ground and had to keep reminding myself to look upwards or to try to position myself so that I was looking upwards.

As I moved slowly away, I looked off to my left. There was a vibrant blue sky in contrast to the lush green grass below. In the distance was a very large rectangular building with mirrored glass windows. In front of and to the left of this building was an enormous "T-shaped" monument. A single column rose up about 60 feet into the air. At the top of the column was a rectangular platform that completed a "T-shape" form. On each side of the platform was a sort of futuristic looking vehicle. There was a statue of a man sitting on the vehicle on the left. He was riding the vehicle, leaning forward in a kind of racing position. The vehicle on the right of the platform was unoccupied and its apparent rider was standing beside it as a racer might stand in front of his car with his racing helmet. I could see astounding detail as I looked at the vehicles, seeing parts of the exposed engine and rivets that outlined the body. I stared for a while in awe of this building and monument, wondering if this was actually a place that existed on Earth that I could later research and find photos of.

After a short time I found myself near a run-down house. I was aware of a very negative vibe from this place and decided I did not want to be there. I tried to leave, but I was drawn closer to the house. I moved up to a wall and realized that once I got close enough, I could see through the wall. I peered into what seemed to be a living room, although it was quite worn and littered with debris. Near the corner of the room, a woman and two kids were huddled together.

I left this place and came to another that was similar to a type of shopping center. I went through a building with a door and there was a truck parked inside, as if on display. I noticed there was writing on the side of the truck. I was happy to see this because I tried to read the writing and was successful, proving to myself that this was different than a dream. On the hood of the vehicle, there was some type of vase. I moved to it and examined it, trying to see if there was writing on it. As I looked, I decided to place my hand on the vase to see if I could touch it. When I placed my hand over the vase, I was surprised to see that my hand appeared pure white and was also translucent. It was almost transparent to the point I could see the vase under my hand. This experience also marked the first time I noticed people were present. It was as if I never noticed them because I was so mesmerized by everything else I was experiencing. When I wondered why there were no people, I started to sense people in my periphery.

During this OBE, I become aware of my physical body and realized my mouth was very dry. This is most likely because I was breathing through my mouth during the experience. Amazingly, I told myself to use my tongue to wet the inside of my mouth. I did this very carefully as I was afraid that it might cause me to return. The reason I did it, however, was so that the dryness in my mouth would not become so much that it would cause me to return. It was my hope that this would allow me to stay longer in the OBE. Something similar happened in my previous experience where I became concerned of my heart rate, possibly fearing something similar to sleep paralysis. During that experience, I paused and listened for my heart. Everything seemed normal in my physical body, so I continued on. In both cases, I became acutely aware of my breathing towards the end of the OBE and decided to terminate it by willing myself back to my physical body. What was extremely fascinating to me about this was the fact I was able to *perceive what was happening to my physical body as well as interact with it* during the OBE.

10:45 am – I lay awake and contemplated the experience. I felt my body was somewhat paralyzed and this caused me some mild concern. In later experiences, I would learn to relish the slight paralysis, feeling as if enclosed in a cocoon of sorts. For now, however, I sluggishly moved my right arm and tried to extend my fingers. A few fingers extended while a couple remained stuck, in their slightly curled position. After flexing them a few times, they were back to normal movement. As I moved out of bed, my entire body returned from sleep fairly quickly.

I was astounded by the experiences. Instead of just traveling to a friend's house to attempt to seek proof that I was actually there, I was involved in a number of fantastic journeys. I had extraordinary feelings and saw things that simply left me in awe. It was immediately apparent to me that, although I would not stop seeking proof, it was important that I should continue on this journey to see where it would take me. These things that I saw and experienced, at least as far as I could tell, were not part of my memories. They were not the stuff of dreams. Perhaps my creativity was working overtime and created all of these strange scenarios. If that was the case, though, why was it necessary to create everything from scratch without using anything from memory at all? It seemed an unlikely possibility.

So, if this was not a concoction of past memories or a completely new fabrication of pure creativity, what was it? Could it possibly be actual travel? If not actual travel, could it be a form of perception we have yet to understand? How was it that I was able to formulate conscious thoughts and decisions during the experience? Why was it that, although I had some control of what I did during my journey, the actual direction of the travel did not seem to be in my full control? How was it that I was able to communicate and instruct my physical body 'remotely' *with the understanding that such interaction could possibly bring me back*?

The questions abounded. Still reeling with the impact of the experience and the possibilities it proposed, I decided to make a record of the event. I immediately recorded a video to recollect and comment on the full experience as best I could. This was the beginning phase of keeping a running journal. Sometimes I would record my experiences on video and sometimes I wrote them down. This way, I could refer back to them and look for clues on how my ongoing journey would change in the future and try to determine the meaning of what it all really meant.

Chapter 10 – What does it mean really?

We are living in the age of scientific reason where the pursuit of precise and verifiable knowledge trumps personal belief, faith and wisdom handed down from the ages. Science provides us with a wealth of information, technological advances and the promise of new discoveries every day. However, because science claims to at least have the capability to explain all mysteries, that which is left to personal experience is left by the wayside. In this way, scientific exploration is relentless in its pursuit, steamrolling a path of verifiable experiments while leaving the unexplained and unverifiable on the edges. To science, these edges become little more than amusing oddities or items to be completely ignored. Those in the scientific community that bravely venture out to examine the edges quite often become ridiculed among their peers or shunned completely. Ironically, the same scientists that ventured outside the norm in the past often made the most ground-breaking discoveries.

Today, blind progress and commercialism also dim our path and indeed, in many cases we seem to be going backwards. For example, consider the big business entities that pharmaceutical companies have become in the western world. Much like many of the medical practices, instead of looking for and promoting cures, they focus on relieving symptoms only. It makes great business sense to sell a product or service that one has to buy over and over, rather than develop a permanent cure. Yet, looking back through history and also in different cultures, we see natural remedies that have been practiced and proven to work for thousands of years. Is this really true progress?

Man has thousands of years of experience of living on the Earth and negotiating the effects of illness, harm and the need to survive the inevitable consequences of nature. He did this without medical science, without corporations and without the support structure that we see surrounding the average person today. Along the way, it was necessary to find and develop solutions to the ills that were encountered. This is a gold mine of knowledge that we seem to be losing more and more of everyday. Today, ancient knowledge, for the most part, is regarded as completely outdated and irrelevant. After all, how could valid knowledge be obtained if it was not discovered via the modern day scientific process and method? Today's conventional wisdom seems to be that 'newer is better'. However, experience tells us that this adage is quite often simply not true.

In the quest for deeper understanding and solutions, our ancestors no doubt not only explored their surroundings, but also explored within. They were not hindered by the multitude of tasks and distractions that color our everyday life, nor did they have vast avenues of knowledge to research. It stands to reason, then, that they would eventually turn to explore their inner self and capabilities. What did our ancestors know and discover about inner travel and the out of body experience? Such experiences would have been important and instead of questioning how it is possible, they would have taken steps to encourage and enhance the experiences. Perhaps they even discovered capabilities and understanding through these experiences that would be incomprehensible to us today. If so, this knowledge appears to be lost to us and it seems that only now some are taking the steps to regain it.

But why is it that such an experience is part of the human condition? Do we indeed have the ability to perceive beyond the traditional five senses? If so, how and why would this perception include realms that we are otherwise not aware of? We also have to ask that, if these are actual places of perception and not products of our mind, what purpose do they serve? Where are they located and what does it mean for the traveler that experiences them?

In my opinion, we still have to take a step back and first determine a way to prove whether or not the experience is a creation of the mind. My reasons are not to question the validity of faith or diminish the experience, but to have a solid platform to explore further. Whether I accept the experience as some form of actual travel or not, it does not prevent me from enjoying and being awed by it. However, having a better idea of how or why it happens can mean a drastic change in your personal exploration. For example, discovering that it is *not* a creation of the mind means opening doorways previously thought impossible. We would have to consider very seriously what it means for us as humans to travel to alternate destinations and to find meaning in the experiences. Is it for our own personal growth or is it something that could affect us all?

There are many, to be sure, that will say that they have definitive proof that they have travelled out of their body. They may claim they have visited a place and have identified things that they otherwise would not have known about. As we have seen, even scientific experimentation has given us some measure of evidence towards proof. In the end, however, there does not seem to be enough to satisfy us all to accept it as fact.

It was my hope while writing this book, that I would discover something that I could bring as hard evidence to present here for your consideration. I have yet to find such proof, but I am confident that even if I did, it would not be sufficient to satisfy those that would remain skeptical. In fact, I'm sure even those closest to me and know my character would question the evidence, if not my sanity. In any event, if I do encounter such evidence in my subsequent travels, it will be a sure reason to either update this book or write a completely new one. However, it may be just as important for us to grow with the understanding that some things must be taken on faith.

So where does that leave us in my quest to understand this phenomenon between the scientific and the incredible? In thinking back and considering a year's worth of out of body experiences, even up to the most recent ones, my travels have been such that I can't imagine that my mind created them. To try to describe the experiences in words is difficult. Even in my journals, I have difficulty to explain the abstract visions and especially the intensity and beauty of the things I have seen. I do not have all the answers that I was so desperately seeking and perhaps that is best. I cannot convince anyone on the validity of my experiences. That is something you have to discover for yourself. But I can tell you this:

In my travels, I have been astonished by scenes of the improbable and unbelievable. I have encountered places that even my dreams could not imagine and have been lifted by a positive force that could shake my very soul. I have come face to face with the unimaginable, descended to depths so fearful that only by the mercy of God was I lifted out and I have soared to heights where I saw, if only for a brief instant, the wings of an angel passing overhead and somehow comforting me on my journey.

I have gazed upon the stars without obstruction of the atmosphere and witnessed ancient cities being built through years of construction even as I glided past them. I have moved among clouds of a manner never before seen on Earth, passed through a mountain that had a system of hundreds of waterfalls and looked upon an ocean that existed upright on a vertical plane.

I have floated in complete darkness while the deepest peace imaginable washed over me. In that time, that mercilessly short time, I knew a comfort unknown on Earth and never before felt in my heart. And once, while floating slowly under majestic trees and looking up at the beautiful stars above, I asked a question without even knowing I was going to ask it. I asked, *Is there anyone there?* And, in response, I felt a sudden and pure energetic force surge through me and shine out from every direction.

And I knew I was not alone.

ABOUT THE AUTHOR

D.V. Nobles has always enjoyed using the creative side of his brain. From an early age, he began writing short stories and put together his own comic books. Later, he discovered the world of music and began writing, playing and producing his own songs as well as music by others. He has been involved in filmmaking, photography and various other artistic ventures. He also enjoys creating 3D models and is owner of blenderfornoobs.com, which offers free tutorials on the Blender 3D software. Always fascinated by the unknown, he was at first stunned by his unexpected Out of Body Experience (OBE) but extremely curious to explore the mysteries that it entailed. It is his hope that his experiences and exploration into this fascinating phenomenon will help others in their own journey into the unknown.

www.ingramcontent.com/pod-product-compliance
Lightning Source LLC
Chambersburg PA
CBHW020512030426
42337CB00011B/353
9780967570419